THE
FIGHTING O'KELLYS

by

Michael E. Ulyatt

HUTTON PRESS
1991

Published by the Hutton Press Ltd.,
130 Canada Drive, Cherry Burton,
Beverley, North Humberside HU17 7SB.

Phototypeset and printed by
Image Colourprint Ltd.,
Anlaby, Hull.

ISBN 1 872167 16 0

CONTENTS

DEDICATION

To Noel O'Connor

ACKNOWLEDGEMENTS

In the summer of 1986, a family friend, Noel O'Connor, suggested I wrote a biography of Con O'Kelly, a Hull boxer who later became a Roman Catholic priest. I had heard of Con but my initial research revealed his father as an equally interesting character and so a joint father and son story evolved.

I am most grateful to the Editors of the Hull Daily Mail, The Stoke Sentinel, The Universe, The Catholic Herald, The Bridlington Free Press, The Goole Times, The Driffield Times, The Holderness Gazette and Boxing News for publishing my original letter appealing for information and photographs. Many thanks to all those who responded to this appeal, especially Bob Larvin of Hornsea; John Hillon of Whitehaven; Tom Clarke of Penmaenmawr; Ray Harris of Upminster; the Rev. Father J. R. Hughes of Loughton; Patrick Myler of Dublin; F. E. Monks, G. Geraghty and C. Sharrocks all of Stockport; Derek O'Dell of Marlow; Mrs. E. Bonner of Bridlington; Eric Wrigglesworth of Hornsea; Mrs. Ada Steele of Birmingham; John O'Hanlon of Liverpool; P. Goldthorpe of Bridlington; the Rev. Father C. J. Roberts of Northampton; Cliff Hornby of Atwick; Mr. Smith of Hornsea; Ian Bulmer of Hunmanby; Canon J. Marmion of Sale; Anthony Lee, John McNally, Miss Shooter, Mrs. McHugh, Wilf Kaye, Arthur Bell and the late Frankie Jackson, all of Hull.

The Boston Globe (U.S.A.) Reference Library, who kindly provided fight press cuttings relating to both Con senior and junior during their respective stays in America; I also received help in my research from the Hull Boys' Club, The British Olympic Association; the Local Studies Library of the Humberside County Council; the Hull Daily Mail Library staff; the Rev. Father Brian Nicholson; Hull City Council Archivist Dept.; the Priests at St. Mary's R.C. Church in Crewe; the Rev. Father Feeney of Alsager and the Amateur Boxing Association of England.

Maureen Foers arranged the typing of my manuscript and Malcolm Fussey copied many of the photographs loaned to me.

Michael E. Ulyatt

The house at Gloun where Con O'Kelly was born in March 1886

Photo courtesy of Denis O'Shea

THE FIGHTING O'KELLYS
by Michael E. Ulyatt

This is the story of the fighting O'Kellys – father and son, devoted Roman Catholics and boxers extraordinaire.

OLD CON

George Cornelius O'Kelly was born in Gloun, just north of Dunmanway in County Cork, Southern Ireland on March 4th, 1886. He grew up to be a sporting fanatic with a great sense of humour, indeed he became known as 'the clown from Gloun' and made an unusual sight, straddling a donkey with his feet dangling just above the muddy path as he made his way to St. Patrick's National School in Dunmanway where he was taught by the Patrician Brothers. Con was tall, broad and fit. He excelled at cycling, wrestling and boxing but never neglected his education. "Big Con", as he had become known throughout County Cork, decided to broaden his horizons and when he finished school he left Ireland and moved to Hull in East Yorkshire, England.

Many Irish immigrants lived in the west end quarter of Hull which was roughly an area bounded today by West Street, Ferensway and Spring Street and Con lived there for some weeks before he moved to lodge with a Mr. and Mrs. Larvin at 9 Blanket Row in Hull's Old Town area. Thomas Larvin was a stevedore on the nearby Hull docks. Shortly afterwards, Con joined the Hull City Police Force on September 18th, 1902 and became Police Constable No. 249, being seconded to the city's Fire Brigade which at that time was jointly run by the Police Force. He was ideally suited for the job, standing 6ft. 3in. in his bare feet with a chest measurement of 50in. and weighing just over 16 stones.

The Corkman was still extremely sports minded and weight lifting was a keen hobby of his. Con once lifted 267lb. double handed and then a single handed snatch of 196lb. However, wrestling was his main sporting interest. A fellow policeman offered to take Con to a wrestling club and the instructor soon realised the newcomer's ability which, together with his impressive physique, seemed to make him a natural. After intensive training, Con was entered into various competitions with great success and he decided to put his name down to wrestle the Northern Counties champion at Liverpool and he beat him in under three minutes. In the next fortnight Con defeated another three opponents and he had improved so much that he was entered for the British Amateur Heavyweight Championships and actually won the title after some great contests.

Con had served four years in the Force when he married his landlord's daughter, Mary Cecilia Larvin, and they moved into a Police house at 58 King Street off Charles Street and near to the Central Fire Station in Worship Street. Most firemen lived in the area and a vigorously rung bell would sound when the men were needed in any emergency. Many a sound sleep was interrupted by that bell! Con became a well known figure riding his double-barred cycle round the city's streets but was well respected. He was involved in an incident on September 6th, 1906 when he had to arrest a man in Charlotte Street and received a vicious kick on the leg. Con still managed to take his prisoner into custody but had to go on the sick list for a couple

Hull Police Fire Brigade at the turn of the century

P.C. 249 Con O'Kelly. c. 1906

of days although he still received full pay.

The O'Kellys' had a son on March 11th, 1907 and they christened him Cornelius after his father. For evermore the two became known as 'Old Con' and 'Young Con'. There was a large Roman Catholic community living in the Charles Street area and Mrs. O'Kelly could rely on help with the family washing and neighbours offered to look after her son, a Mrs. O'Malley would often take the baby out for a walk in his pram. Mrs. Fallon also helped the family.

Old Con continued his amateur wrestling career with the Hull Amateur Wrestling Club in his spare time but his training schedule was severely curtailed when a gable wall fell on him on March 4th, 1908. The brigade had been called out to a fire at Frank Soulsby's saw mill at the corner of Thomas Street and Hedon Road early in the morning and Con was tackling the fierce blaze together with a Sgt. Veal, P.C. Newman and P.C. Hynes when the 20ft. high wall collapsed at the two storey building and the four firemen were completely buried under the rubble. Their other colleagues frantically dug them out with their bare hands and the quartet were taken to the Royal Infirmary in Prospect Street. Con was the only one of the four to be detained and he spent several days in the Infirmary with a severely bruised back and shoulder and many cuts on his face. He was off work for 27 days and received £5/15/8d from the Employers Liability Assurance Corporation but despite this bad accident, Con was soon wrestling again, although he lost his British Heavyweight Amateur title to Edmond Barrett of Listowel and a member of the City of London Police A. C. Amazingly, Con's recovery was complete when he was selected to wrestle for the United Kingdom in the freestyle or 'catch as catch can' heavyweight section (weight over 73 kilograms) of the 1908 Olympic Games held in London. The wrestling section was held in Shepherd's Bush and Con was drawn against an American, Lee J. Talbot, in the first series. Con put on a leg hold and an arm hold and he beat him in just one minute and ten seconds. The renowned English wrestler, Harry Foskett, was beaten in the second series. Foskett first tried for a leg hold and Con got behind and tried a neck and crotch hold. Changing to an arm and crotch hold he turned a half nelson and won in 4 minutes 5 seconds. In the third round Con met his old rival Edmond Barrett and won amid great excitement with an outside stroke, lifting Barrett off his feet and putting on a further arm and crotch hold, winning in 2 minutes 14 seconds. This win qualified the Corkman to meet the great Norwegian matman, Jacob Gunderson, who was the Scandinavian and American champion. Con gained another magnificent victory. It was described in the official story of the Olympic Games:- 'O'Kelly at once brought his opponent to the mat with a neck hold, then putting on a half-nelson and crotch hold but the Norwegian released himself. O'Kelly again slipped on a half-nelson but Gunderson, turning in, countered with a leg and arm hold. O'Kelly secured top position and won with a wrist hold and half-nelson in 13 minutes and 27 seconds. In the second bout, O'Kelly brought his opponent down from a forward hold and chancery. He then pulled his man backwards and brought him to the mat with a body hold and press down in 3 minutes and 35 seconds'. Con had done it! He had become the first Irishman to win an Olympic Games gold medal at wrestling. It was a very proud Con O'Kelly who received his medal from Queen Alexandra and after she had whispered her congratulations, the Queen gave him a special green oak-leaf badge in recognition of his great feat. By coincidence, the winner of the free-style lightweight section

Con in the 1908 Olympics

Con in wrestling pose after his Olympic win

Con is chaired by his Fire Brigade colleagues from Hull's Paragon Station on his triumphant return to Hull on 27th July 1908

Con's triumphant procession reaches the Worship Street Fire Station

gold medal and runner-up in the free-style middleweight section in the same wrestling finals was George de Relwyskow representing the United Kingdom and he was to promote wrestling contests in Hull for many years after.

News of Con's victory soon reached his adopted city and when he returned to Hull the very next day together with his trainer Mr. Atkinson, over 12,000 people were waiting to greet him at Paragon Station. On the platform were his wife, together with the Chief of Hull City Police, Major Malcolm; the Chief of Worship Street Fire Station, Supt. Booth and Chief Inspector Bailey. Con was sporting a white skull cap decorated with the Union Jack and wearing the green oak-leaf badge which Queen Alexandra had presented him with, the competitor's medal in his lapel and his gold winner's medal was tucked away in his pocket. After greetings from the official welcoming party, Con was lifted and chaired aloft by six burly colleagues from the Fire Service to cheers from the huge crowd. He was carried to a chemical fire engine, patriotically decorated with Union Jack flags and drawn by two horses through the city centre to the Worship Street Fire Station where he received another great reception from his work colleagues, all of whom had taken the Irishman to their hearts.

After this magnificent show of public support, Con had to make decisions in the following weeks which were to change his life completely. He received several offers to wrestle on the Music Hall stages throughout the U.K., offers which, if accepted, would have certainly affected his work as a fireman. However, Hull's adopted citizen saw his future in professional wresting and Con applied to Hull's Watch Committee for leave of absence to meet Jose Levette, professional wrestling champion of Spain but to Con's dismay, the Committee turned down his request and Con reluctantly decided to tender his resignation, so keen was he to continue his ambition to become a champion in the professional world of wrestling. For their part, the Watch Committee unanimously accepted his resignation on February 3rd, 1909. He was later to be publicly thanked for bringing so much publicity to the city of Hull and in turn Con said he always tried to do his best as a P.C. and regretted he couldn't make some of the kids on his beat "a bit more decent. They even pinched my helmet once and I never did see it again!"

The O'Kelly family had to vacate their police house and on the 25th February they moved by handcart and rully to 77 Waverley Street, just two doors off Con's in-laws, the Larvins. Con was now training in earnest and in his first professional wrestling bout he met John Lemm in a world heavyweight title contest at the Oxford in London, where despite gaining the first fall, Con was beaten. After this bout, Con wrestled Eugan Sandow, Tom Cannon and the famous Georges Karl Julius Hackensmidt of the U.S.S.R., who was undefeated between 1900 and 1911.

When Con wrestled the Russian, in the words of a spectator, "Hackensmidt dusted the auditorium with O'Kelly, throwing the Irishman regularly without any bother at all". Con won his next three contests, beating John Lane in London for the Great Britain Championship when he gained the decision in just two minutes and ten seconds. His next opponent was Andrew Markovitz, champion of Romania and Con gained the first two falls in 14 minutes and 11 minutes. In August Con beat Jimmy Essen in a bout scheduled as the "Championship of Great Britain and Ireland" for a £100 purse and Con won two falls out of three.

The Corkman was challenged to throw six local heavyweight wrestlers inside

Wrestler Eugan Sandow, who actually promoted the products of Hull firm W. T. Owbridge in 1897

thirty minutes in a mid-week charity matinee at the Alexandra Theatre (at the corner of Bourne Street and George Street) in Hull. Police Chief Inspector H. G. Duck (senior) trained five of the wrestlers, all who worked on the city's trams and who had taken up the sport for enjoyment and as a way of keeping fit. The sixth matman was a Walter Colley. Duck was later to become Chief of Hull City Fire Brigade between 1931 and 1935 but despite all his training and advice, Con took only 12 minutes to dispose of all six. The proceeds from the event went to St. Vincent's Roman Catholic Boys' Organisation, then in Wright Street and where Con was later to found a gymnasium and train boys in the noble art of self defence as well as wrestling and general keep-fit. Among the local artists appearing that night at the Alexandra Theatre was Billy Richardson "who gave a rendering of boiled beef and carrots on what was said to be the largest stage in the provinces." Billy worked for Holmes Tanners in Campbell Street. At another charity matinee, Con played a gladiator in a scene set in Ancient Rome and he was dressed in a loincloth, raising many laughs from the packed audience with the delivery of some of his lines including these:- "Noble Sayzer, the haythen champion lies defayted at your fayte". Would Julius Caesar have understood the Irish brogue?! At a third charity show the Superintendent of Norfolk Street Police Station, Charles Hopkins, blacked himself up to wrestle Con in a match billed as the World Championship of Great Britain and the Rest of the World, but Charles sweated so much the colouring came off him by the middle of the first round!

Con was also very keen on a boxing career and on one bill at Hull City Hall he was proclaimed as "the future heavyweight boxing champion of the World", certainly a most optimistic statement by the show's promoter E. Holloway. His opponent was the American Tom Kennedy who had previously beaten Frank Moran, Al Palzer, Jim Savage and drawn with 'Gunboat' Smith. The advertised purse of £750 was said to have been the largest purse ever given in the North of England. On the same bill were Seamen Eager (Brighton), Harry Curley (London), Private Hewitt (R.A.M.C.) and local fighters Kid Hagon, Jerry Matthews, Percy Wilson, Gordon Jones, Joe Moore, Horace Barker, Charley Rhodes, A. Allison and W. Gladstone. Seat prices ranged from £1 down to 1/- (5p) and the Waterloo Prize Band played for two hours before the tournament. The fight itself was scheduled top of the bill for twenty rounds but it did not go the distance because the referee disqualified Con for butting although the Irishman was adamant that Kennedy was also responsible for butting. Con decided around this time to try his luck in American wrestling circles and early in 1910 he travelled by ship to Boston and took lodgings there. He would like to have met the American wrestler Frank Gotch, champion of the world, but on the advice of the famous boxer Bob Fitzsimmons, Con took up boxing and fixed himself up with former world light heavyweight champion Tommy Ryan as his manager. Con had managed only one wrestling match when he met Pat Connolly in New York but the police intervened and stopped the match after forty minutes on the grounds that the contest was nothing but a rough and tumble fight.

Ryan had Con train at the Pastime Gym on Syracuse North Side every afternoon for three months. Con's weight was 225lbs. and his measurements were:- Height 6ft. 4½ inches; Chest 52 inches; Waist 35 inches; Thigh 25 inches; Calf 16 inches; Neck 19½ inches.

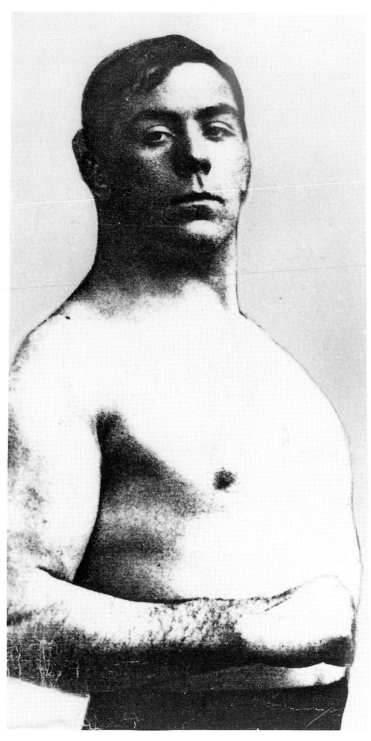

Con was tipped by his American manager Tommy Ryan to beat heavyweight World Boxing Champion Jack Johnson if he maintained his excellent progress

Con before his first fight in America against Con Comiskey in 1910

Con's first fight was in July 1910 and he knocked out Con Comiskey in two rounds and then he knocked out Joe Cowne in three rounds in Utica, New York. Further victories were gained over Al Williams in eight rounds at Syracuse; Bill Edwards in eight rounds; Buck Smith again in eight rounds, at Oswego. On November 10th Con lost his one and only fight in America when Hank Griffin beat him on points over ten rounds. Griffin had twice drawn with Jack Johnson and although past his best, he was too clever for "The Harp", as the 24 year old Corkman was sometimes referred to by the local boxing sports writers. However, Con gained his revenge when in the return match, he knocked out Griffin in the fourth round. Tommy Ryan, who had trained Jeffries, thought Con would make a great fighter, his attributes being his great strength and willingness to learn. "He keeps himself fit by careful living and although I don't want to predict too much, he has the physique to go all the way to the top in boxing".

On January 13th, 1911 Con met Jeff Madden before a crowd at the Rink, New Bedford. Con was billed as "the white man's hope" and the fresh-faced Irishman, although lacking the science, did all the leading. Madden had Bob Armstrong and Billy Pearce in his corner and they saw their man skip around the ring, dodging the clumsy O'Kelly. Undefeated middleweight champion Tommy Ryan was handling Con and he had Bob Barry as one of his seconds. In the fourth round Madden opened a cut over Con's left eye and referee Patsey Downey took a long look at it but allowed the fight to continue. Both men slugged it out and Con put Madden down for a count of five in the tenth round. Despite his bad cut, Con finished the fight strongly but the referee called it a draw, by general agreement if both men were standing at the end of twelve rounds then a draw would be declared. Before the fight Bob Lefavor of Brockton had issued a challenge to the winner. Sam Langford, resplendent in fine clothes, derby hat and dandy cane was introduced to the crowd when just two weeks later Con met Porky Flynn on the Onondaga A. C. bill at a packed State Armory in Syracuse. A crowd of 2,500 were seated and another 500 standing. Bob Armstrong was in Flynn's corner and his man opened the cut which Con had suffered only two weeks previous with a right jab in the first round. The cut bled throughout the fight but Con landed the most effective punches and Flynn soon sported bumps under both eyes. Con was behind on points early on (a usual occurrence) but from the sixth round the Corkman took over and shaded the rest of the fight. It had been a fast and furious bout, reckoned by the locals to have been the best heavyweight contest seen in the area for many years.

Con was obviously learning fast and becoming more skilled in his boxing defence and he gained the verdict ahead of Flynn over ten rounds.

On February 28th Con met Jim Barry of Chicago in a ten round exhibition bout on the Onondaga A. C. bill in Syracuse. Barry is said to have "toyed with the burly Celt and could have knocked out his taller and heavier opponent at any time in a fight more resembling a burlesque but he seemed to want to give the spectators value for money and so prolonged the fight". By the sixth round, the crowd had seen enough and they booed and hissed the fighters and many left the ringside. Also on the bill were Howard Morrow, Joe Argen, Hank Massel, Henry Keibel and Jimmy Lyons.

Con later beat Jeff Madden twice, over ten rounds and four rounds and his final fight in the States was a no-decision bout against Jim Perry.

His American tour had made him financially sound and whether it was home

St. Patrick's Roman Catholic Church in Spring Street, Hull. August 1988

sickness and the realisation he was missing his family, Con decided to return to England. He had made many friends in the Boston and New York areas. "Americans live for their boxing and I've met some swell people. God bless you all. I hope to return some day", he told a local newspaper reporter on his departure. Con's record in America was twelve fights, nine wins, one draw, one defeat and one no-decision.

Back in Hull, Con was to become a father again, his daughter being born in 1912 and baptized as Mona at St. Patrick's R.C. Church in Spring Street, Hull. This Church was consecrated in 1904 and several engraved silver plaques dedicated to the O'Kelly family members are still there. Con carried on boxing for a while. Silas Alger of Plymouth managed him for a time and after Con had lost on points to Jim Johnson over eleven rounds, he wanted a return in Bordeaux but Alger refused to fix it, saying "no, cut out the coloured men" and he issued a challenge through the Sporting Life to Bombardier Wells, Jack Mahoney or Gunner Moir in June 1913.

The National Sporting Club invited Con to be at the ringside when Wells and Mahoney met in London on June 30th, 1913.

Con had victories over Corporal McFadden, knocking him out in two rounds; Dennis Haugh in two rounds and Bomber Legassick also in two rounds. Further wins over Cyclone Warren and Gustav Marthuen were recorded before the big Irishman announced his retirement from the ring in April 1914. He had been running the Grapes Public House in Brook Street for two years, combining the two careers very well. Beer then was only $2^1/_2$d (1p) a pint! He had been an instant hit with his customers, many being of Irish descent. He had always enjoyed a good yarn and was keenly interested in local shipping matters, probably because of his father-in-law's business interests on Hull docks. One evening the pub door was pushed open and a large, well dressed man entered and came up to the bar in obvious distress. "Excuse me sir, but where is the urinal?". Con stroked his chin thoughtfully and glanced up at the oval clock above the bar. "Um, the urinal eh? Well to be sure, I know the Melbourne Castle will be in the river about now and the Union Star will be sailing on the next tide but I've never heard of the Urinal. Is she a British ship, sir?". Exit one man muttering strong oaths about the unhelpful Irish! On another occasion, a man hardly taller than the bar top came in and asked Con for a pint of mild. The publican took a glass from the shelf behind the bar and as he bent down over the pump to draw the beer, the little man picked up the poker from alongside the fireplace and raising it high, he hit Con over the head. He then dropped the poker on the floor and ran out of the pub. The blow only dazed Con and he never did find out who the man was and why he had hit him.

The family gave up running the pub in 1915 and moved to a large house at 67 Freehold Street, off Spring Bank and Con opened a pot and crockery shop nearby and he also owned some property which gave him a comfortable living.

Meanwhile, Old Con had finally retired from the wrestling and boxing rings at the age of 29 and he realised a long held ambition by opening his own gymnasium at the rear of his house. Young boxers he trained there included Syd Wass, George Shooter, Stan "Young" Squares, John McDermott, Fred Wilby, Tommy Gorman, George and Ralph Henderson, Tommy Walton, Len Donnelly, Tony Lee, Eddie Pollard and George Hart. Unfortunately Hart tragically died when he met a Cardiff boxer at Hull's Assembly Rooms and he struck his head on the canvas and never regained consciousness.

Old Con was still a very fit man and apart from guiding young boxers he could 'skip on a sixpence for fifteen minutes'. His son now had a keen interest in boxing, which was hardly surprising considering his father's passion for the sport. "Come on lads, train hard and learn – it's good for the soul. Use yer energy and make yourselves into a man" Old Con would exhort his young charges.

Old Con with his son (second right) and three of his other young charges. c.1921

YOUNG CON

In 1912 Young Con started school at St. Patrick's R.C. School in Mill Street. It was run by the Sisters of Mercy and Con was remembered as a slightly built child in short trousers which were about three inches above his knee. He had a reputation for chasing the girls around the small playground and pulling their hair.

Young Con had moved school at the age of eight to St. Charles' R.C. School in Pryme Street. He soon fell foul of one of the teachers, Miss Maggie Ryan, who was forever berating him for lack of attention in class before she found out he was short sighted, so he had to wear glasses and sit at the front of the class. When he was twelve, Con played Rugby League for his school but only once as his teacher realised he was big for his age and so his opponents would have been in mortal danger from his physique.

Old Con must have been as pleased as punch when his son made his first appearance in a competitive fight in the 7 stone class at the Sailors Children's Home, Cottingham Road, Hull at Whit in 1919. Arthur Bell fought on the same schoolboy bill. "I remember Jimmy Fallon, Bill Ruston, Joe Phillipson, "Wacker" Wilby, Tommy Gorman and Johnny Miller (later a Police Chief Inspector), all keen boxers". A classmate of Con's at St. Charles' R.C. School was Ted "Tarzan" Tarling and they met in the Northern Counties schoolboy final at Hull's Beverley Road baths. Tarling won and brought the silver trophy to school next morning. Con was later to win the 7st. 12lb. schoolboy boxing championship in 1920. Around that time, a group of St. Charles' boys took some scrap iron from a nearby foundry and were taking it back to school one lunchtime. What they didn't realise was that they were carrying 'live' detonators and they were banging them against a wall in Pryme Street near to the Irish National Club when one of the detonators exploded with a vivid orange flash and three of the boys were killed instantly, Jim Howlett and two called Mann and Anderson. Confusion and panic spread and one of the St. Charles' teachers sent Young Con and Arthur Bell to tell Howlett's mother in Freehold Street of the calamity. One of the bodies was laid in a huge wicker basket used to display pots outside a nearby crockery shop.

A year later Young Con left school shortly after he had won the 10st. 8lb. schoolboy title. He continued his education at Eton Court, a private school in Albany Street, Hull run by a Mr. Mortimer Petty, M.A. Mrs O'Kelly wanted Con to study to become a lawyer or a doctor but he wasn't a bright scholar and was much more interested in boxing as a career. His former schoolmates used to pull his leg and run off with his black school cap. They were lucky if Con didn't catch them as he was in regular training at St. Mary's Boxing Club in Wilton Street where he was coached by Billy and Paddy Mills, at a gym near a farm in Marfleet and at a barn in Stoneferry where kerosene lamps were used to light the ring. In face of all this keenness on boxing, Con's mother reluctantly agreed to let him finish his studies early and train virtually fulltime. He boxed all over the country with his dad in the corner, aided by George Shooter. George was a family friend and many schoolboy boxers in Hull were to be grateful to him for his training, patience and enthusiasm for the 'noble art'. Old Con worked for a time as a dock foreman for his father-in-law's stevedoring business. His feats of strength during this time became a legend and many dockers marvelled at his timber carrying efforts.

Young Con was growing into a fine athlete, indeed one of his former schoolmates, Wilf Kaye, had joined the Merchant Navy and while on leave he bumped into Con in Bond Street in Hull's city centre and failed to recognise him because Con had filled out so much.

At the Hull Boys' Association championships at Wenlock Barracks, Con beat S. Wass where the ringside scribe reported "he won because of his greater experience and ringcraft". His boxing career was now really taking off. He won the North of England amateur light heavyweight title in Sheffield in 1924 when he was sixteen years old and in the same year he reached the A.B.A. Finals at Alexandra Palace in London, losing to 'Fireman' Billings in an entertaining fight. Con won the Tailteann Games heavyweight championship. In February, Con beat W. Wildsmith of Sheffield at Hull Boys' Club when he knocked his opponent down early in the first round and his opponent did not come out for the second round.

All this activity brought Con to the notice of the British Olympic Selectors and he emulated his father by being selected for the 1924 Olympics, a unique father and son Olympic double.

The VIIIth Olympiads were held in Paris and there were nineteen entries in the heavyweight section, but only sixteen competed. Con was Great Britain's second string, with A. J. Clifton of the Port of London first choice. Con fought Bertazzdo of Italy in the first round but lost on points. The Italian lost to O. Van Porat of Norway, the eventual winner. Con later gave his Olympic blazer to his uncle, Bob Larvin and it remained in the family for many years. After the Olympics, Con's father suggested he turned professional and also that the family move to Burton Road, Hornsea. In their short time there, the O'Kellys became friendly with George Hamilton Smith who had a coal merchants business. He was to become a valuable second in Con's corner in the next few years.

While they were in Hornsea, John McNally (son of Sgt. McNally of Hull Boys' Club fame) sat behind Con in church one Sunday morning and marvelled at the thickness of his neck.

Old Con proved to be a shrewd manager and he fixed up his son's first pro fight on home territory at Madeley Street Baths off Hessle Road. His opponent was Ike Clarke of Birkenhead and the fight took place on November 14th, 1924. The fight promoter was Mr. E. Holloway and Billy Corlyon was the timekeeper. A crowd of over 1,000 saw the bout get off to a slow start and referee Curly Osborne had to tell both men to box. O'Kelly, cool and workmanlike, landed right and left crosses and Clarke gasped when a right hook caught him in the ribs and then Con knocked his opponent down and the Lancashire man's corner threw in the towel in the fourth round. A victory in his first pro fight was greeted warmly by the crowd and the O'Kelly entourage.

Con's bustling, no-nonsense style soon made him a big favourite with boxing crowds. He was to fight fifteen times in just twelve months, fighting in Hull, Belfast, Manchester, Liverpool and Newcastle.

Madeley Street Baths was also the venue for Con's second fight against Sonny Lonz Webster on December 12th after Eddie Pearson of Bradford withdrew at short notice. The original terms were for £25 a side plus a purse. The referee stopped the fight in Con's favour in the thirteenth round after both fighters had taken a lot of punishment. The show was promoted by Mr. E. Holloway and entrance fees were:-

Old Con with his son on the right and Bob Carvill of Bridlington on the left

"Fighting fit". Young Con. c. 1924

Stage Chairs 8/6d., Ring Chairs 5/9d., Outer Ring 3/6d., Balcony 2/4d., Body of Hall 1/2d. Tickets were sold at Suggs, the Tally Ho! Public House and Fulford Hall. Seven local fighters were on the support bill, Tom Walton, Tommy Gorman, Ted Jacobs, Billy Baker, George Bennett, Tom Gunstead and Smut Stephenson.

Con's next fight was against Ellis Powell of Leeds on January 19th at the Lyric Theatre, Anlaby Road, Hull. The 25 years old West Yorkshireman weighed in at 13st. 6lb. and stood 6ft. 1in. Terms were £25 a side plus purse on a "winner takes all" basis. The medical officer was Max Lucas and the referee Harry Dorsey. A large crowd at the Lyric contained an unruly element and when the fight started Con seemed a little nervous. Once underway, he landed several heavy punches, so much so that his glove split in the third round and the fight was stopped for a change of gloves. Con had Powell down for a count of nine in round four and floored him twice for counts of eight in round five and his seconds threw in the towel. Powell had lacked a good defence but both fighters looked tired. Local boxers on the same bill that night were Len Donnelly, Ted Jacobs, Tom Walton, Young Jackson and J. Thompson.

Two weeks later Con met local fish merchant Harry Moody at the Lyric Theatre. A capacity crowd paid prices between 2s. 4d. and 8s. 6d. The fight referee was Mr. J. Farnall of Liverpool. Con started off the fight well and Moody had to take a lot of punishment to the body and by the seventh round he had had enough and his seconds threw in the towel. "He was too good and far too strong for me" said Moody, who years later was to become a fight promoter. Also on the

Young Con wearing his Olympic blazer with his friend George Gray.
Bridlington 1924

*A signed photograph from Young Con to George Shooter, one of his trainers
in Hull*

Madeley Street Baths in Hull where Young Con fought fifteen times

31

bill that night were Len Donnelly, Tommy Gorman, Billy Young, Billy Thorold, Charlie Holloway and Smut Stephenson, all local lads.

Con's next opponent was Gunner Bennett of London who he met at the Lyric on February 16th when the referee was Mr. H. Jennings of Bradford. Con's father and Gordon Jones were in the Hull man's corner and they saw their man in action straight away with rights to the body. Bennett made good use of the ring and landed several uppercuts in the second round and also gave Con further punishment in the third and fourth rounds. The Londoner was warned for illegal use of the head and honours were even in the tenth, eleventh and twelfth rounds but although Con was the heavier puncher, Bennett was proving to be the better boxer until the referee disqualified him in round fourteen for persistent holding, a decision which was very unpopular with the crowd. Local boxers on the same bill were Johnny McDermott, Billy Mills, Len Donnelly and Harry Moody.

Stoker Stubbs of Portsmouth, the light heavyweight champion of the Channel Fleet, met Con on March 2nd at the Lyric. The referee was Jimmy Wilde, the great Welsh flyweight and world champion from 1916 to 1923. He received a real Yorkshire welcome when he entered the ring and after the preliminaries, the fight got underway at 8.45 p.m. The large crowd were soon cheering Con, who coolly landed several punishing blows. Stubbs was soon in trouble from repeated body punches and although Wilde cautioned Con twice for using the back of the glove, the Hull man was too strong for Stubbs and by the end of round eight he had taken enough punishment and the Portsmouth man retired. Len Cutts of Howden together with Hull boxers Dick Clarke, George Baker, Jack Townsend, Harry Esplin and Tommy Gorman were all on the same bill. After the fight, the evergreen Jimmy Wilde came down to Con's dressing room. Con was on the massage table but quickly sat up and listened attentively as Wilde offered some sound advice. "Now look you. I watched your efforts closely tonight and you must have hit Stubbs twenty five times right on the spot but not hard enough to knock him out. You should hit straight with the front of the glove, not with the back, the heel or the palm. Don't keep your hands clenched all the time but make a tight grip just before the blow connects. You are a heavy lad and powerfully built but you didn't punch your weight tonight. Put more snap into your punches, give 'em a crack like this" and Wilde drew his arm back and let it go again in the old piston-like style, straight into Con's ribs. Con grunted as he signified he had felt the blow. Jimmy, nicknamed the "ghost with a hammer" in his prime, also passed comment on Con's stance and method of advance, advising him to go straight in and finish the job quickly.

Fourteen days later, on March 16th, Con was again in action at the Lyric, this time against the Newport fighter Trevor Llewellyn. The Welshman had a height and reach advantage but Con started hitting harder than his opponent and landed some sledgehammer blows to the body. However a left to the throat sent the Hull man reeling on the ropes and he looked in real trouble but Con recovered well and counter attacked, leaving Llewellyn with a cut mouth by the fourth round. Two rounds later he was unable to defend himself and the referee stopped the fight. It was Con's best performance to date. On a good boxing programme, local lads Harvey Heron and George Bradley were on the supporting bill.

Con gained an easy win just three weeks later when he met Stanley Glen of Bethnal Green at the Lyric. The tall Londoner took a hefty left to the body and a swinging right to the jaw which put him down for a count of seven and when he got up a left to the chin knocked him clean out, all in just ninety seconds. A sparse crowd showed their disgust at Glen's poor performance.

Con's next fight, his ninth, was his first outside his native city when he met Len Brookes of Horwich at Liverpool Stadium. The 18 year old was given a gruelling fight but impressed with his power and gameness after being hit low three times. Con went down after the first low blow and would have gained the verdict if he had stayed down but he staggered to his feet only to be put down in the fifth, again by a foul blow. Incredibly, the referee only cautioned Brookes but after yet another low blow in round seven, he did disqualify him and declared a very sore Con the winner.

George Hetherington of Bishop Auckland was Con's opponent at St. James' Hall, Newcastle on September 28th. The Hull man was much heavier than his opponent and although Hetherington gave Con some heavy punishment, he soaked it all up and came back strongly to gain the verdict when the referee disqualified Hetherington in round nine for persistent holding.

A packed audience at the Artillery Barracks in Park Street, Hull on October 5th saw Con meet Kid Moose, billed as the heavyweight champion of Canada. Con himself appeared on the bill as 'the coming champion of England'. Moose had visited the Hull Daily Mail offices the day before the fight, together with his manager and he said how confident he was that he could win. The doors opened at 6.45 p.m. and local lads on first were George Lawson (having his first professional fight), George Darley, Billy Rewston, Harry Heron and Len Donnelly. Before the main bout, a Mr. Rhodes gave an exhibition of concertina playing!

The referee was introduced as the Canadian Tommy Burns, heavyweight Champion of the World in 1906. He said he had come to referee the contest according to the rules of boxing and hoped the best man would win. The timekeeper was Billy Corlyon of Hull. In the opening rounds Con took a lot of punishment but gave as good as he got. He put the Canadian down in round thirteen with a left uppercut but there were calls from the crowd for him to stop leaning on Moose. At the end of fifteen rounds, Con gained the verdict on points, a decision which received a mixed reaction although referee Burns later said he gave the Hull man the decision because he did most of the forcing.

Con's next bout was against Dick Power of South Wales at the Free Trade Hall in Manchester on October 13th. Power scored almost at will in the opening rounds with some accurate straight lefts and he had opened a cut under Con's right eye in round one. The Hull fighter had no defence that night and a big surprise came when he knocked out the Welshman in round three. Boxing experts at the time thought if Con did have an obvious weakness it was in his defence and he attempted to eradicate this with special work-outs, paying attention to ducking, countering, guarding and slipping before his next fight on October 21st against Jack Phoenix of Dublin at St. George's Market in Belfast. Con and his father left Hornsea en route for Belfast via the Liverpool ferry, calling in at the Hull Daily Mail offices before boarding the train at Paragon Station. It was Con's thirteenth fight and his superior punching power gained him the verdict when the referee stopped the fight in round four after the Irishman's seconds threw in the towel during the referee's count.

The Hull fighter gained a ninety second knockout against Harry Gold of London on November 3rd at Manchester's Free Trade Hall. Even in so short a contest, Gold

Clovelly, the O'Kelly's former family home in Trinity Road, Bridlington.
July 1988

received a warning for holding but four left hooks left him reeling and a left, right combination sent him through the ropes. Gold was suffering from an acute attack of boils but the Sporting Chronicle reported "Both hands were brought into play by O'Kelly, who hit very hard and must have landed a score of punches before the Hebrew slipped through the ropes and onto his back".

The O'Kellys moved their family home about this time, ten miles further up the east coast to Bridlington. Old Con soon had a gym organised in some old stables in Trinity Mews at the bottom of their garden at 'Clovelly', 19 Trinity Road. The three storey house was so large the family had a maid, named Ada. She remembers Mrs. O'Kelly telling her son "If you're going down the garden put your overcoat on, it's a bitter easterly wind tonight".

After fourteen successive wins, thirteen inside the distance, Con met his first pro defeat and in front of his home town crowd at Madeley Street Baths. His opponent was Charlie Chetwynd of Leicester. Before the fight began a masked "raiding party" organised a Poppy Day collection, as it was Armistice Night. Referee Ben Green of the British Boxing Board of Control started the fight at 8.50 p.m. and it was all action straight away. Both men took a lot of punishment but Chetwynd used the ring more until he was floored by a right hook in round thirteen. The Leicester fighter finished the stronger and there was no doubt his greater experience gained him the points decision at the end of fifteen rounds. It had been a great fight and the audience had loved it. Local boxers on the same bill were Charlie Holloway (the promoter's son), Johnny Brown, Kid O'Keefe, Bill Wall, George Darley, Arthur Wilkinson, Harry Moody and Tom Cooper.

Twelve days later, Con was to fight for the first time at the National Sporting Club in London, where professional boxing in England was governed between 1891 and 1929. His opponent was Joe Mullings of Catford and the fight took place just three days after the death of Queen Alexandra, who had presented Old Con with his Olympic gold medal over seventeen years previous. Mullings had also been beaten by Chetwynd and he was no match for Con that night, taking two counts of eight early in the fight and two more counts of nine in the third round before the referee stopped the fight. Con had shown great coolness and determination with excellent footwork and strong body punching.

The first draw of the Hull man's career was against Jean Leroi of Belgium on December 2nd. It was Con's second fight at St. George's Market in Belfast, a top of the bill contest. He started off in whirlwind fashion and despite his opponent claiming a foul blow to his neck, Con had him down four times in quick succession and it looked all over after seven rounds. However Con stopped using his powerful right hand for some reason, probably because of injury and Leroi made a terrific comeback to share the spoils after fifteen action packed rounds. Newspaper reports of the Pact of Locarno being signed grabbed the headlines from the fight the next morning. The O'Kelly party made their way home from Ireland by ferry and train and just thirteen days later Con met Gunner Bennett of London at Manchester's Free Trade Hall. It was Con's third contest in Manchester but not an impressive one. He was reduced to being described as "little removed from the novice stage". A left hook put Bennett down in the ninth round and he slipped getting up whereupon his second entered the ring and the referee had to disqualify him. The promoters afterwards announced that Bennett had broken his contract by boxing at Birmingham on the previous Monday and his share of the purse was withheld and donated to charity.

On January 25th, 1926 Con fought for the second time at the National Sporting Club when he met Jim McDonald of Salford. A family friend, Eric Wrigglesworth of Hornsea was in the Army based at the Tower of London and the O'Kelly party invited him to the fight but Eric was unable to obtain leave. His family had once run a horse drawn carrier business from Hornsea to Blanket Row, in Hull's Old Town where Old Con had once lodged. Con had been scheduled to meet Marine Trinder on Boxing Day but had to withdraw with ear trouble. Trinder couldn't meet the re-match date because he had already signed a contract to meet Loop Liet so the N.S.C. brought in Frank Fowler of York until Old Con revealed a local promoter had already matched his son with Fowler and so McDonald came in as substitute. O'Kelly, being much heavier, was too strong for his Lancastrian opponent and boxed him out of the ring and his seconds threw in the towel in round four to end a one-sided contest.

Con was now training very hard and putting in a lot of sparring practice and roadwork around Bridlington, where he had many fans. When Mrs. O'Kelly visited her local butcher she bought five steaks. Although glad of the business, nevertheless the butcher asked her why five when there were only four in the family. "Because Con eats for two and he also has six eggs for breakfast", Mrs. O'Kelly explained.

Con's next four fights were all at Madeley Street Baths. On February 2nd he met Paul Journee of France in front of a packed house. The former heavyweight champion of France visited the Hull Daily Mail offices on the day before the fight and was observed to be "a massive man, in the pink of condition". The Lord Mayor of Hull, Coun. Frank Finn, was present at the fight and Billy Corlyon organised a collection for the family of Dick Clark, a local boxer who had died that week. Referee W. J. Farnell of Liverpool got the fight started at 9.15 p.m. and it soon became obvious the Frenchman was "too slow and beyond the best age for boxing" according to the Hull Daily Mail's boxing correspondent. The crowd began taking the mickey out of him and Con put him out of his misery in the second round after knocking him down four times with powerful body punches. Also boxing that night were Billy Rewston, Young McHugh, Len Donnelly, Arthur Hewitt, Paddy Welch, Sid Wass, Jim Spivey, Tom Gunstead and George Lawson, all local lads.

Two weeks after this fight, Con was in action again, meeting Jean Leroi of Belgium for the second time. It appeared to be a well-matched contest but Con was to suffer the second defeat of his career. It was a clean punching contest throughout and referee Farnell gave nine rounds to Leroi, only three to Con and three level pegging. Leroi received a great reception from the sporting crowd, in fact both fighters got a standing ovation. Old Con quickly fixed up a return bout at £100 a side and a purse. This took place on March 2nd and there were few vacant seats available when the Lord Mayor of Hull, together with the Sheriff of Hull, local councillors and many important people from the business and sporting community attended the Baths and accorded both men a noisy welcome. O'Kelly waded in from the start and it was a tough fight. A vicious right to the throat put Leroi down in the fifth round and he was very weak-kneed before Con finished him off. It was a confused Belgian who shook hands with Con, giving a Continental type shrug of the shoulders.

A sparse crowd was evident at the O'Kelly and Marine Trinder fight on March

22nd. Prices ranged from 2/4d. to 10/6d. The Portsmouth man suffered a lot of punishment and he was down from a right uppercut in the second round and again in the third from a right to the stomach before being knocked down three times in the sixth and twice in the seventh. A body punch put him down once again in round eight and his seconds threw in the towel. Referee Jennings raised Con's arm as victor, his twentieth success.

On April 30th, 1926 Con fought on the same bill as the Phil Scott (Holder) and Boy McCormick contest for the Heavyweight Championship of Great Britain at the King's Hall, Belle Vue, Manchester. The purse was a massive one of £1,400. Con's opponent in one of the supporting contests was Charlie Smith of Deptford. In the fight programme notes Con was described as "a youthful heavyweight sensation, still in his teens, who although no stylist, is a very thorough workman who hits very hard. Very shrewdly managed by his father, O'Kelly is expected to go very far in the boxing game, especially when he has mastered the science of defence". Smith had a most unusual style, coming in very open with hands stretched apart but he had a highly effective defence. He conceded weight to Con but had an advantage in height, reach and boxing knowledge and after fifteen gruelling rounds, Smith was given the verdict by a narrow margin, his experience and superior boxing skill being decisive. It had been a great fight, even better than the championship bout.

Con had a three month layoff following this fight and he didn't box again until August, when, determined not to lose a fourth fight, he met Stoker Stubbs of Worksop over fifteen rounds at Leeds Stadium, a new boxing venue. Extraordinary crowd scenes gave rise to an invasion of the ringside seat area which had to be cleared before the fight could start. It was a tough fight but Con was given a clear points decision and he was a popular winner. His reward was a ten week break from boxing after he had fought twenty five times in twenty two months, a very busy fighting record.

Con met Stubbs for the third time on October 18th, this time at York and his left hooks and jabs to the head were matchwinners and although Stubbs was a game trier, Con's superior punching won him the fight when he knocked out his opponent in the ninth round.

Twelve days later Con met George Hetherington for the second time, this bout took place at the Spa in Bridlington for a purse plus £25 a side. Con was in fine punching form and he knocked out the Bishop Auckland man in round three. A solitary cry of "foul blow" was later denied by both referee Jennings and Hetherington. Local boxers Ted Moss, Pat O'Keefe, Harry Heron, Johnny English, Young Jackson and Sid Wass featured on the same bill together with Bridlington favourites Bob Carvill and Arthur Simpkins. Coun. A. E. Gray presented a silver trophy to Patsy Carvill, winner of the eight stone competition.

A fight billed as the "Irish Championship" was Con's next outing in the ring against Dave Magill at Madeley Street Baths on November 15th and it drew a large crowd. A right to the jaw put Magill down for a count of nine early in the fourth round and he was saved by the bell. Con rushed his opponent through the ropes in round seven but was himself knocked down for a count of two in round ten, the first and only time Con was legitimately knocked off his feet in his entire career. He was now very weak and taking a lot of punishment, so much so that his father decided to throw in the towel in round eleven but unfortunately it landed on the ropes, unseen by the referee. Magill quite rightly kept on punching Con to the head and body. Old Con experienced a fierce protective attitude and leapt through the ropes in an attempt to restrain Magill, whose seconds intervened and held their man back, thus averting a nasty scene. Old Con apologised later to the referee and to the Magill camp, an apology which was immediately accepted all round.

Con's first fight in 1927 was at Cleethorpes against Stoker Miller of Portsmouth, the reigning Imperial Services champion. It was described as one of the best fights in North Lincolnshire for some time. Miller took a lot of punishment from his heavier opponent and won only two of the fifteen rounds but he stuck to his task although Con's victory had been expected.

The former Middleweight Champion of Europe, Gus Platts, was Con's next opponent at Madeley Street Baths. The Sheffield man was elusive throughout the fight and there were only light exchanges early on. Con was the aggressor throughout the contest and referee J. Hulls of London had no doubt about giving a points decision to the Hull man. A sparse crowd gave Platts a big ovation as he left the ring.

Eleven days later Con was scheduled to meet George Slack of Doncaster but he was injured in training and Tom Fowler of London stepped in as replacement. A large crowd, attracted by the original billing, were at the Central Rooms, Scunthorpe and they saw plenty of in-fighting early in the contest but sharp punches shook Fowler badly and despite bleeding from the nose he gamely fought on but went down for the full count in round four from a left hook to the head and a fierce right to the body.

Just one week later Con was in action again, this time in his adopted town of Bridlington. Before the fight against Fred Young of Marylebone, Con received a £50 or £100 a side challenge from Jack Hankinson of Northwich. Young had a weight, height and reach advantage and started the fight aggressively, being warned for using his head. Con feinted for the body and threw a left hook and a right to the jaw to knock out Young in the first minute. The crowd at the Spa were delighted. Young's manager offered another fight for £100 a side. Con senior accepted the offfer subject to satisfactory terms being agreed. The delighted O'Kellys walked the mile home discussing future offers.

Will Lancaster of York signed to meet Con at York on March 14th over fifteen three minute rounds. According to the Sporting Chronicle's report "O'Kelly was always on top, possessing the longer reach. Lancaster punched strongly but had a weak defence". He couldn't keep Con away and the referee warned him for leaning. He was very relieved to hear the bell at the end of round four and found five but a right swing to the body finished him in the sixth and Lancaster retired. He was subsequently found to have a fractured rib.

The German-Jewish boxer, Ted Sandwina, was Con's next opponent on March 30th, at the Royal Albert Hall, London. On the way down to the 'smoke', the O'Kellys were involved in a car crash and although not hurt, Con was certainly shook up. Mrs. O'Kelly was very worried about her son's condition and suggested to her husband that Con should pull out of the contest. He would have none of it and boxed a draw over ten rounds although most critics thought he could have won. During the fight the Prince of Wales entered the hall and received a hearty reception, as did both boxers at the end of a tremendous fight. The undefeated German was managed by his mother, reputedly the strongest woman in the world! Her son had won all his previous fights within the distance and although scientific boxing in this contest was not seen, the hard hitting contest brought an enthusiastic audience to their feet. A re-match was quickly fixed up after the fight, again at the Royal Albert Hall but a hand injury forced Sandwina to withdraw and Gunner Bennett stepped in at very short notice. Supporters from Hornsea, Hull and Bridlington made the long trip from Yorkshire to London and they were not disappointed by the night's events. Con completely outboxed his opponent and, while not over-exerting himself, hard body punches left Bennett gasping and the referee stopped the fight in the fourth round. In the next weeks Con received offers to box in Australia, South Africa and America, all of which were seriously considered by father and son on the journey back home. They eventually decided on another year in England to give Con a chance of winning the British Heavyweight championship before trying their luck in America.

Con fought for the third successive time at the Royal Albert Hall against a now fit again Ted Sandwina. It was a poorly attended event at first but filled up eventually with many well known boxing celebrities in attendance. It was the second fight on the bill. Sandwina was the more skilful boxer but it was mainly long range stuff and although Con got through his guard several times, his blows did not land. Referee Sam Russell gave the verdict to Sandwina on points after fifteen rounds. The defeat was a bad blow to the O'Kelly's plans and they took stock over the next two months before a fight with the Swedish boxer John Strand was fixed at the Metropole in West Street, Hull. The Yorkshire Sports Syndicate promoted the bill which included George Darley and Young Pullen of Hull. Prices were 2/4d., 3/6d. and 5/9d. but a disappointingly low gate saw the Swede fight well for the first five rounds but a badly swollen eye restricted his boxing ability and referee Harry Dorsey of Leeds stopped the fight in the eleventh round in favour of the Hull boxer. Another eight weeks of hard training was Con senior's orders before a visit to Nottingham to meet Battling Sullivan of Wales. It was a mis-match really as Con battered Sullivan into submission by the third round. He was down from a right to the chin for a count of seven, then again for a count of eight and then floored by a terrific right to the ribs before the Victoria Baths crowd urged the referee to step in and stop it, which he did.

Con was very keen to meet Dave Magill so that he could avenge his defeat suffered just twelve months previous. Before the fight at Madeley Street Baths, Roland Todd issued a challenge of £100 a side to Con, which O'Kelly senior accepted. A full house saw a greatly improved display by Con and although the first two rounds were close, Con had Magill in trouble in the third and fourth rounds and an accidental clash of heads in the fifth saw blood pouring out of the Irishman's forehead. The back of Con's glove had caught him above the eyebrow as the referee ordered them to break and Magill's seconds threw in the towel in the sixth round. Referee Harry Dorsey raised Con's arm as victor and Magill needed two stitches in the cut after the fight.

Three weeks later, Roland Todd's challenge was taken up and the York man, a former European Middleweight Champion, came to Madeley Street Baths full of confidence. There was much in-fighting through the contest with Con scoring points from left hooks and lefts to the body, countered by Todd clinching and then jabbing to the head. After fifteen rounds, Harry Dorsey gave it as a draw, a decision which the large crowd certainly did not agree with as they thought the local man had done enough to win it.

1928 was to be a momentous year for twenty year old Con. His first fight of that year was against Tom Berry, ex-Cruiserweight Champion of Britain. A crowded Madeley Street Baths heard Harry Crossley of Mexborough challenge the winner and they then gave both fighters a great reception in the ring. Before this, local lads Jack Townend and George Darley were on the support bill and Rugby League players Andrew Carmichael (Hull Kingston Rovers) and George Tootles (Hunslet) met with Tootles winning in the eighth round.

When the O'Kelly and Berry fight started, both men were cautious. Berry threw his best punches early on before O'Kelly started to mix it. Exchanges were even throughout and although Con was warned by referee Dorsey for a low blow in round ten, he got the verdict on points after fifteen round. Berry's management were very keen on a re-match, their man receiving a great reception when he left the hall.

Jack Sharkey was scheduled to meet Van der Veer, champion of Holland, in a fifteen round contest at the National Sporting Club in London on January 30th, but Sharkey had to withdraw shortly before the fight with an injured hand and Con deputised at very short notice. It proved to be a very strenuous fight with both men wary of each other in the opening rounds before Con boxed well to get himself out of trouble but the Dutch champion was taller and heavier and the Hull man took some heavy punishment. Con then scored well himself with several upper cuts and then he hurt Van der Veer with a vicious left hook in the twelfth round and then the Dutchman was warned by the referee for holding. The large crowd were very appreciative of both boxers' efforts in the final when Con's clever footwork and some tremendous counter punching gained him a narrow points victory. He returned home to Bridlington the next day and was given a great reception. Under the circumstances the fight against Harry Crossley at Madeley Street Baths six days later could have been cancelled but Old Con decided that his son could meet the challenge. It was a lack-lustre fight however, even though Harry Dorsey gave a count of eight against Crossley in the first round but tiredness was Con's biggest problem and the fight drifted into a draw. The verdict seemed to be a fair one but the large crowd were not pleased with the announcement. On the same bill that night were Bob Carvill of Bridlington and "Battling Sullivan", Joe Smith, Arthur Wilkinson and two Hull lads, Tommy Gorman and George Darley. Four years later, Crossley was to lose a British light-heavyweight title fight with Jack Petersen, the Cardiff fighter.

The French heavyweight champion, Leon Sebilo, came to Madeley Street Baths on February 27th. The fight started at 8.45 p.m. and referee J. King of Middlesbrough had to separate both fighters early on in the fight and then the Frenchman claimed a low blow. He was warned twice for illegal use of the head and by the tenth round he had a badly cut eye which later needed two stitches. Con was probably ahead on points when the referee stopped the fight in round eleven because of Sebilo's bad cut. The sporting Hull crowd gave him a great reception and he was very keen for a re-match. Harry Crossley had issued a further challenge before this fight for £100 a side and best purse offered.

The Deptford heavyweight, Jack Stanley, came to Madeley Street Baths on March 19th. It was to be Con's last fight at the Hessle Road venue and he had

Young Con shortly before his first trip to America in 1928

previously fought fourteen times there, winning nine, losing three and drawing two. Stanley visited the Hull Daily Mail offices the day before the fight and was reported to look very fit. Con had finished off his training three days before and then went for long walks to Sewerby over the weekend followed by massages at home. When the fight got under way, both men boxed cautiously before Stanley got through Con's guard in the third round. Neither man seemed to hear the bell sound for the end of round six and in the ensuing confusion, a second was knocked down. Round Seven saw the crispest despatch that a Hull boxing crowd had seen. O'Kelly delivered a tremendous left and right to the chin which put Stanley out for the count. Also on the bill that night were Hull boxers Billy Foley, Hewitt, George Lawson and 'Young' Squires.

Con's career record was now thirty six wins (thirty inside the distance), five defeats and four draws in just forty months of a hectic programme. It was in the summer that a family conference decided that his fighting career was at a crossroads and perhaps they should try their luck in America. For probably the first time in public, father and son met in the boxing ring, at a garden fete in aid of St. Vincent's. On July 14th they left Hull, together with Bridlington boxer Reg Brown, for Liverpool en route by liner across the Atlantic to their Boston base on the eastern seaboard of America. Old Con did ask both George Shooter and George Smith to join them on the trip as joint trainers but both men had to decline, Shooter because of his commitments to his young family and Smith because of his coal business in Hornsea. Before leaving home, Con had plenty of sparring practice with Joe Jackson, George Lawson, Jack Miller, Johnny O'Connor, W. Mills, T. Walton and the Gorman brothers, Jim and Gus. The local boxing community wished the O'Kellys well in America, as did the many Catholics in Hull and the East Riding. Old Con had relatives living in Boston and also had many acquaintances made during his previous stay there. Their landlord was a Nottingham man who had moved to Massachusetts forty years previously and Old Con was to have many conversations with him about the 'old country'. Old Con was a wily bird though, realising there were many Irish Americans living in the Boston area and to gain their support, he unashamedly announced his son as the 'Heavyweight Champion of Ireland', thereby increasing his box appeal. He was soon looking for a manager for his son and fixed him up with Tom O'Rourke, who had a lot of fight contacts throughout the States. In his letters home, Old Con asked to be remembered to Teddy Goldstein, Mr. Bannon, Mr. Green and the "crockery and pot men in the Open Market!". Con started full training at Grupp's gymnasium on New York's 116th Street in September and he impressed ex-welterweight champion, Jack Briton, who thought Con was a marvellous protege for his age (just 21). Tom O'Rourke paid sparring partners between five and ten dollars but the Hull man "knocked four bells out of them all. He's really fit and rarin' to go" said his father and after watching several fight bills, he wrote home "Gorman would have made a fortune out here, they love a gutsy fighter". Con's first fight on American soil was against Al Friedman, a scheduled ten rounder at the famous Madison Square Gardens on November 5th. "I loved ducking through the ropes at the Gardens – what an atmosphere. It was a great feeling" said Con later. The 'roly poly Irishman', as the press had started to call him, won on points and two weeks later he met Jack Gagnon in the Mechanics Building in Philadelphia and again won on points over ten rounds. Organised by the

CON O'KELLY
HEAVYWEIGHT CHAMPION OF IRELAND
TOM O'ROURKE, Mgr.
1465 Broadway, N.Y.C. Phone WIsconsin 1941

Young Con after his arrival in America

A Christmas greeting from Young Con to his friends in Hull from America, 1928

PROGRAMME

❈

FRIDAY, DECEMBER 21, 8:15 P. M.

FIRST BOUT—4 ROUNDS

BRUNO		FRANK
SALA	*vs.*	**CAWLEY**
Greenwich Village		Philadelphia

SECOND BOUT—6 ROUNDS

HARRY		EDDIE
SMITH	*vs.*	**PFISTER**
Harlem		West Side

THIRD BOUT—10 ROUNDS

YALE		TOM
OKUN	*vs.*	**KIRBY**
East Side		Boston

FOURTH BOUT—10 ROUNDS

TUFFY		CHARLEY
GRIFFITHS	*vs.*	**BELANGER**
Sioux City		Winnipeg

FINAL BOUT—10 ROUNDS

JIM		CON
MALONEY	*vs.*	**O'KELLY**
Boston		Ireland

Top of the bill at Madison Square Gardens in New York, December 1928

Sharkey A.A. Club, Con had weighed in at 192$\frac{1}{2}$lbs. and Gagnon was just $\frac{1}{2}$lb. heavier. The referee misheard the bell at the end of the second round when Con had Gagnon at his mercy. Con showed remarkable speed and class and he won nine of the rounds. The referee was Joe O'Connor, the judges Dave Nelligan and W. T. McDermott and the timekeeper Denny White. Also on the bill were Big Boy Rawson of Boston, Ray Thompson, Ownie Flynn, Eddie Benson, Hambone Kelly, Ted Johnson, Laddie Lee and Johnny Cucio. Boxing correspondent James O'Leary described Con as a "fine, handsome physical specimen, such as one could imagine the late John Boyle O'Reilly to have been at his age. He outclassed Gagnon in every way, showing himself to be a fast, clever boxer and gave promise of a brilliant future in the ring". The large crowd gave Con a great reception. He had landed four blows to every one that Gagnon threw.

Con then had a month before his next fight when he was top of the bill against Jim Maloney, pride of South Boston, at Madison Square Gardens in New York. Con weighed in at 193$\frac{1}{2}$lbs.. six pounds less than Maloney and veteran announcer Joe Humphries sent them on their way with the words "and may the best Irishman win". Maloney carried the fight to O'Kelly from the opening bell and in the second round he opened a cut above Con's right eye. Con came back strongly in the third round with brisk jabs and swift hooks and he won the round and the next one too but he then lost the next three as Maloney peppered him with right and left combinations. The Boston man was warned for a low punch in the eighth and this incited Con to fight back. He was better fighting at long range. The fight ended with both boxers standing toe to toe, slugging it out and the 10,000 crowd (who had paid nearly 35,000 dollars) thought that Maloney had won the fight but possibly two warnings for holding and a low punch, went against him and a draw was given at the end of ten rounds. On the same bill was Gerald Tuff Griffiths of Chicago who beat Charles Berlanger of Canada just weeks after being knocked out by James J. Braddock of Jersey City. Con was now attracting attention from American fight fans and a month later he met George Gemas in Syracuse and hammered him into submission when the referee stopped the fight in the third round.

It was Con's massive frame pounding down Boston's Huntington Avenue which drew the attention of sportswriter LeRoy Atkinson one week later when he had a re-match with Jim Maloney at the Boston Gardens. "I was impressed with the young man's modesty and he clearly thinks he can win. His father, standing head and shoulders above his son and weighing probably fifty pounds more, has a ruddy complexion and with his big wing collar, he could have just stepped out of a clothing store window in Dublin. The big men from the land of Shamrocks certainly stood out in a crowd". Atkinson asked Old Con about his son's success in America. "He is getting in better condition and although he has been punished hard he seems to be taking it and he's not flinched yet. You could say that he's a chip off the old block!". He was also asked if he boxed with his son. "I used to, to be sure, but not now. He might remember how I used to tap him and he might let me have one!".

Both Con and Maloney trained at the same gym the day before the fight, although at different times and a big Friday night crowd was predicted. Tipped as the best Irish heavyweight since the days of Jim Coffey, the Roscommon giant, Con fought another strong fight but suffered his first defeat in America and his first set back in thirteen fights over a period of eighteen months when he lost on points over ten

Young Con signed this photograph to his friend, George Gray of Bridlington,
on his holiday from America in the summer of 1929

rounds. After this fight, Con should have fought Max Schemeling but the German backed out and he never forgot that snub.

Two weeks later Con was again in action in Boston, this time against Ernie Schaaf, who was disqualified in the sixth round. Con then lost three consecutive fights, the first on March 4th when he lost on points to Matt Adgie over ten rounds in Philadelphia. After this fight, Con's Irish cover was blown when George S. Renwick of Boston wrote to the Sheffield Telegraph's "Green 'Un" in England to enquire about Con's background and the newspaper gave the O'Kelly's full family and sporting history. Whether this expose upset Con is unclear but he then lost to Harold Mays of Bayonne, New Jersey on points over ten rounds at the Arena in Philadelphia. Mays, a sparring partner of Gene Tunney before his two fights with Jack Demsey, had weighed in at 181lbs. seven pounds less than Con and he proved too clever for the wild swinging O'Kelly.

Eleven days later, Con met Jim Maloney for the third time in four months, this time for a staggering £3,000 winner's purse in a top of the bill clash at Madison Square Gardens in New York. Maloney battered Con into submission and although he stayed upright, the referee stepped in to stop the fight in Maloney's favour in round three.

After this disappointing turnabout in their fortunes, the O'Kelly's decided to return to East Yorkshire for a well-earned holiday during the summer and early winter of 1929. Con's pro record was then fifty four fights, forty wins, nine defeats and five draws. Back home, he kept up his strict disciplined training and boxed exhibition fights at the Floral Hall in Hornsea against Paddy Welsh and Charles Hellyer for charity. Also in action that night were Jack Townend, George Darley, Arthur Wilkinson, "Young" Thompson, George Martin, George Naylor, Mark Monkman, Reg Brown (who had earlier left the O'Kellys in America and returned home to study and he qualified later as a doctor), Harold Usher, "Young" Elliott, Arthur Hornby and Kid Prescott. Old Con refereed all the contests with great enthusiasm. While home on holiday, Con visited the St. William School in Market Weighton, a reform school administered by the Christian Brotherhood. There was a fine boxing gym there and Con and his father became regular visitors, advising inmates of the skills and boxing. Con was eventually asked to become a patron of the school together with his father. Old Con finally persuaded his wife to return to America with them and his daughter Mona and an aunt went too. They sailed from Liverpool to Boston on the White Star Line's s.s. 'Cedric' in February 1930. Young Con wrote to his friend George Shooter in Harrow Street, off Hessle Road from on-board ship. "The crossing has been a bit rough but the O'Kelly family were fine sailors and not seasick". Some of the passengers were not to Con's liking, "one or two will get a dressing down if they are not careful. I'm just longing to get my hands on someone. They are all puffs!" This time accommodation was obtained in Dorchester, Massachusetts. Old Con wrote home to George Shooter, telling him that "Mrs O'Kelly felt the cold at first but she is feeling warmer now as the house has no fire but warm air heating throughout means the house is never cold – it's remarkable". Con worked out in the gym with George Cook from Australia. Fighters were being paid £6 to £10 for an ordinary four round preliminary fight, a lot of money then. Con trained very hard, sparring with Jimmy Rogers, Bob Sharp, 'Sandy' Jack Taylor, Pat McArthy and also Ted Moore from England. He hit too hard for any of them to continue for many days and he was in great shape. He was back in action again on June 17th, nearly fourteen months since his last fight. His opponent was Jack Dudley at Portland Maine and Con was in no way ring rusty, despatching Dudley in seven rounds. The O'Kellys were in demand socially in Boston and it was another two months before Con met 'Tiger' Tom Dixon, again in Portland Maine and he knocked him out in eight rounds. Six weeks after this fight, 'King' Solomon of Panama was the Englishman's next challenger in Portland Maine and this was a much harder fight. Con gained the decision with a narrow points victory after twelve tough rounds. He was really at his peak as a fighter now and proudly wrote of his success to George Shooter in Harrow Street, Hull but asked "What's become of Bob Carvill?" His old man always used to tell me the crowds only came to see Bob and not me. Well, I don't think that's so now. I hear Bob has been judging beauty contests in Bridlington. Now, what's a fighting man doing, judging women's ankles?" The two rivals never did meet in the ring professionally. It was rumoured that their fathers made a pact that it wouldn't happen and they asked their respective second to honour that agreement should anything happen to both fathers. Old Con had managed Carvill's affairs at one time, as well as looking after Con's interests.

On Tuesday October 21st, Con met Jackie Gagnon over ten rounds in the Boston Arena. It was nearly two years since Con had beaten him but this time the result was reversed although a large section of the crowd did not agree with the decision. Con received a magnificent ovation from the crowd on leaving the ring and the boxing correspondent of the Dorchester Beacon said local fight fans would be clamouring for a fourth match against Jim Maloney. If Con had won that night he would have met Henry La Mar and the winner of that fight was scheduled to be matched with Jack Sharkey, known as 'the Boston Crab' and who was to become world champion in 1932.

Con then met Al Friedman in Boston in a contest which was red and raw from the first bell. The Rosindale fighter turned Con's left eye crimson early on and the 3,500 crowd went wild. A draw would have been the fairest result but the Massachusétt Boxing Commission did not allow such decisions and probably because Con had finished the last four rounds in style, he was given the nod at the end of ten rounds. Just fifteen days later Con met Michele Bonaglia in the Boston Arena, and won that fight on a third round disqualification. It was a welcome win and boosted Con's confidence. He then had two months off, training daily though and then being matched with 'King' Levinsky over ten rounds at the Boston Arena but lost on points, a decision so unpopular that the crowd booed the officials for a full fifteen minutes after the result was announced.

A month later, Harold Mays was Con's opponent at Portland Maine but a no-decision ruling at the end of the sixth round finished that contest. Con then had a disastrous run of six fights without a win. In July he fought a draw with Giacomo Bergomas over ten rounds at Madison Square Gardens and then lost there to the same boxer in a re-match in August when Bergomas was given a points decision after ten rounds. A defeat by Tuffy Griffiths on points over ten rounds in Chicago, a decision which the normally sporting Old Con later described as a "travesty, a terrible decision" was followed by a battling draw over ten rounds with 'King' Levinsky in Chicago. Two defeats in a month further dented Con's confidence. At

Young Con on his return from America in 1931

"Elmpark" on the road to Macroom in County Cork. September 1986.

Photo courtesy Denis O'Shea

51

"Elmpark" on the road to Macroom in County Cork. September 1986.

Photo courtesy Denis O'Shea

Minniapolis he was defeated by Dick Daniels on points over ten rounds and he lost in the same manner to Baxter Calmes in Chicago. Con's fight record in America from November 5th, 1928 to April 19th, 1929 and June 17th, 1930 to October 26th, 1931 was twenty three fights in twenty three months, with nine wins, ten defeats and three draws and one no-decision. He had slipped down the listings but several close decisions had cruelly gone against him. The O'Kellys had no grumbles though. Boxing in America was a tough business and Con's long time weakness at in-fighting was constantly being exploited. Cruel fate now took a hand in the family's affairs. Con's sister Mona, who often accompanied her brother on his training walks, was taken ill suddenly with appendicitis and tragically died at the age of 20. The whole family were devastated. They had always been close and they immediately made plans to return home and the funeral took place in Cork. On his arrival back in Hull, Old Con told a Hull Daily Mail reporter, "the death of my daughter was a very great blow to us all. Mona was a very fine girl. I lost interest in everything for a while. Her death completely altered our plans so here we are back in Hull". Young Con's plans for his boxing career were unclear but there is no doubt that Mrs. O'Kelly strongly requested him to hang up his boxing gloves. Eventually the family decided to sell up at Bridlington and move to Southern Ireland. They bought a poultry-rearing farm at Elmpark, on the road to Macroom and Killarney in County Cork. Old Con had a setback in his new life when, trying to get away from a chasing turkey, he fell over a log and unfortunately broke his leg. The O'Kellys never settled in their new life, missing their many friends in the East Riding of Yorkshire and so they returned to England. The family decided to re-settle in Sale in Cheshire and Con, who had kept himself reasonably fit but had put on weight began to talk seriously with his father about making a comeback to the ring. With so much time on his hands, Con realised that at the age of 29 he ought to do something positive with the rest of his life.

It was said that he had already decided to enter the Roman Catholic priesthood after many serious conversations with his mother and father. His earnings from the ring had left him a comparatively rich man by 1930's standards but he had bought the family house and provided for his parents' comforts. Because of his dwindling bank balance, Con did not want to become a burden, financially, on his church if he decided to become a priest and so he decided on making a boxing comeback to possibly finance his studies.

He was to fight six times before retiring from boxing forever. Con began serious training in April 1937 and his ringcraft and stamina needed some hard work on his part. His first come-back fight was on September 22nd, 1937 against Bert Ikin of Birkenhead at Hull's White City. Ikin had trained for the fight across the River Humber in Grimsby and caught the paddle steamer across the River for the fight. Young, tall and strong, it was thought Ikin would prove a good test for Con. At the weigh-in at Sugg's in Paragon Street, both men weighed 14 stone. Jack Smith was the referee and when the fight started, Ikin immediately landed three good solid punches but a swift counter attack from Con and lefts to the head resulted in Ikin being unable to see properly out of one eye. By the third round, his seconds felt that their man had taken enough punishment and threw in the towel. Ikin apologised to the crowd from the ring and explained he couldn't see out of one eye. A large crowd gave Con a great ovation but there was some booing at the result. Jack Carrick and

Con O'Kelly, the family pet lover

Con O'Kelly, the family pet lover

Con Flynn were on the same bill. Considering it was his first fight in six years, Con felt pleased with his own performance. Two weeks afterwards, Con fought at the same venue against Max Hodgetts and he won in five rounds when his opponent retired. It was to be Con's last appearance in the ring in his home town. He had fought twenty five times, winning twenty, losing just three with two draws. Con's father then approached the London promoter Sydney Hulls with an offer to replace Delaney in his proposed fight with Strickland at Harringay when it was rumoured Delaney would have to pull out of the fight. Hulls turned down the idea but promised to pencil in Con for a future Harringay promotion. Hulls, together with his brother Jim, assisted their father in promotions at Crystal Palace. Sydney was for a time matchmaker for Arthur J. Elvin at Wembley but left to conduct his own matches at Harringay. However, nothing materialised for Con. He did get a crack at the vacant Northern Area heavyweight title, which, in true "Boys' Own" style, he won by beating Harry Lister of Tynemouth on points over fifteen rounds at Manchester's Free Trade Hall. Seven weeks earlier Con had fought Jacob Schonrath and won on points over ten rounds at Liverpool Stadium.

On February 17th, 1938 Con met Erwin Klein at the Liverpool Stadium. His giant opponent was a bit of a disappointment and Con got the verdict on points after ten rounds. He scored many points with his famed left jab, which had proved so successful over many years.

Just five weeks later, Con boxed his last professional fight when he was matched with the Canadian heavyweight Cal Rooney over eight rounds at Liverpool's Anfield Football Stadium. A crowd of over 40,000 saw the top of the bill fight between Benny Lynch (World, European and British Flyweight Champion) and Peter Kane, a contest which Kane seemed to dominate throughout but a draw was the verdict in the non-title fight. Con weighed in for his final bout at 13st. 10lb. with Rooney over a stone lighter at 12st. 8lb. It was a tough contest from round one and there was little to choose between both men until the final two rounds when Con took the fight to Rooney and that tipped the scales in Con's favour. A section of the crowd booed the decision but most ringside observers felt it was correct.

Shortly after this fight, Con announced his retirement from the ring. It was said that he was annoyed at not being fixed up to meet Tommy Farr and that the proposed purse for a fight against Reggie Meen, known as the Desborough Giant, was not big enough. A more likely reason was that Con had finally decided that at the age of 31, the time was right to begin his studies to enter the Roman Catholic priesthood. Informed boxing enthusiasts at the time considered that the British Heavyweight title had been his for the taking if he hadn't gone to America. So ended a fighting career which had spanned fourteen years and his record stood at 74 fights, 51 wins (37 inside the distance), 15 defeats, 7 draws and 1 no-decision. He was only legitimately knocked down once in his career. He had been on the fringe of success on both sides of the Atlantic but didn't quite rise to the height of his potential ability, probably because his height and reach were just not enough for a heavyweight champion. "He was great at going forward but not so good at close defence" said one leading boxing writer who had seen many of Con's fights. Con had graced the noble art and could be proud of his chosen career. He had been a tough, uncompromising fighter who had never known when he was beaten, who had always given of his best and who had trained hard for all his fights, giving boxing crowds real value for money entertainment. Now he could put away his gloves and boots and begin plans to start his studies. In August 1939 he helped take some lads to the St. Vincent de Paul camp at Rhyl in Wales and boxed the cook using flour bags as gloves! The lads loved it.

Young Con (seventh from the left, middle row) at Campion House, Osterley in the early 1940s

Young Con (first left, back row) was an Air Raid Precaution Warden at Campion House, Osterley in 1941

FATHER CON

Con began his studies at Campion House, Osterley. John Hillon, a fellow student at the time, recalled "Con was a father figure to me during the early 1940s. He was a wonderful character with a terrific devotion to Our Lady". John joined the RAF during the Second World War and did not resume his studies for the priesthood after the War. Another fellow student described Con as a "jolly, kind person with a sincere disposition and he had an earnest desire to become a priest. He would often visit Irish friends in London during his time off". During the War years Con was an Air Raid Precaution Warden at the College and did excellent work with the civil authorities connected with the military. He would even "dig for victory" most afternoons in the Campion House vegetable plot. A senior priest put him in charge of the chickens. When one of his "brood" was not well, Con would perform a gentle operation, slitting the birds crop to find the cause of the trouble, clear it out and then sew it up again. He had massive hands but was very gentle. One fellow student at Osterley tried to stir Con's anger on a number of occasions but Con was wise enough never to rise to the bait. "I knew what he was trying to do but I never lost my temper to give him any satisfaction". Con's great physique was much admired by his fellow students and at their request he would sometimes relate his boxing history but only to a few close friends in the common room after evening prayers. "I was only afraid of one man in my boxing career and that was my dad because he could beat me!". At times his friends would ask him to let them try to punch him. "Yes, go on, punch me on the nose" and then that person would swing a punch but Con would sway slightly to one side and the swinging fist would miss its target. On a serious side though, Con was no scholar and found his studies hard going but he struggled on. "I worked all through the holidays at my Latin to pass my exams the following term". His natural ability for disciplined work paid off though and Con did pass and he eventually moved to study further at the Beda, which had been evacuated from Rome to Upholland in Lancashire because of the War.

Con had put on a lot of weight after years of regular training and his studies had severely restricted any time at all for training. He now smoked a pipe occasionally and was unofficial masseur to 400 students in Lancashire, a popular exiled Tyke.

On May 10th 1945, Con was ordained as a Roman Catholic priest by the Bishop of Shrewsbury at Bishop's House, Shrewsbury and he was celebrant at his first Mass at St. Patrick's Church, Hull on the following Sunday. Mr. and Mrs. O'Kelly must have been very proud parents and they presented him with his first chalice. Con would have liked to have stayed in Yorkshire and did express a desire to remain in the Middlesbrough Diocese but the Church authorities would not agree to his request.

Con was often asked by parishioners and priests alike why he had given up boxing to become a priest. He would reply with a slight smile on his face "Well, it must be like falling in love. Your wife may not be the most attractive girl in the world, she may not have a lot of money and yet you still fall in love with her. Why? You probably couldn't tell me, could you?".

Con's first parish was at the Church of Our Lady and the Apostles in Shaw Heath, Stockport. In his clerical collar, black suit and black trilby, Con looked exactly what he was, a minister of religion but one of his first acts when he became curate at Our

Father Con in happy mood

Lady's was to start a boxing club for the lads in the parish. The club was held in the Memorial Hall in Flint Street and Con's first message to his parishioners was to get their children involved. "It will keep them occupied and off street corners. An opportunity for clean, healthy entertainment and exercise, a place where boys can spend their leisure time building a healthy mind in a healthy body, a centre for the practice of controlled physical exercise which stimulates the mind and provides a safety valve for excess energy. A place where boys can improve their growth, mentally, physically and morally, a place where character as well as muscle will be built and finally a club to train a boy to become a good citizen as well as a good boxer".

Vincent Higgins of Stockport told me this story:- "At school in the late forties we had a teacher who was a bully. He was 6ft. tall and I'm sure as wide, he gave us hell. One year as Christmas came around, we all went into the church hall for the Christmas party. In the centre someone had put a boxing ring. We lads forgot the cakes and minerals. Who was going to box? The time arrived, we sat excited. The first man into the ring was "the Bully", then it was announced he was fighting our hero, Father Con. He was just in boxing shorts and had boxing gloves on, what a change from always seeing him in his clerical clothes. Anyway, he was our hero. You can think of Roy Rogers, Kit Carson or the like but Con was ours. 90 boys sat around the ring. They both started and then in the last round our hero let go with an uppercut. Oh yes, it missed the teacher by about a quarter of an inch. For the first time I saw fear on a man's face. Within minutes the fight ended, the headmaster stepped

Father Con with the Rev. Kevin Molloy at the Church of Our Lady and the Apostles. c. 1946

Father Con was a popular figure at the Church of Our Lady and the Apostles where he ran a boxing club for boys in the Parish, helped by an enthusiastic committee

"Do it this way lads" advises Father Con at training

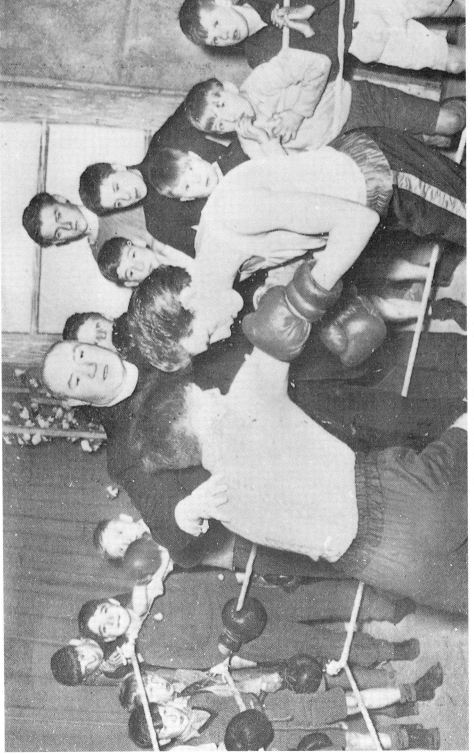

Break! Father Con at training

Playtime fun with Father Con

into the ring. He announced a draw. We boys did not agree, we said our hero had won. Of our teacher, well he never bullied again . . . as a result the former bully became a better teacher, we boys began to respect him, so I consider at the end of the day, no one lost!"

Con organised a contest against a Catholic Boys' Club in Liverpool and took his place in the Stockport's lads' corner in an off-white polo neck jersey with a white towel thrown round his neck and carrying a plastic bowl. In between bouts, a member of the crowd asked him what had been his hardest fight. "Becoming a priest, lad" chuckled Con. In the very next contest, the Liverpool boxer crossed himself with the sign of the cross before the fight began. "Will that do him any good, Father O'Kelly?" asked the Stockport boxer. "Not if he hasn't done any training, lad. Get out there now and get at him straightaway" was Con's advice to his young charge.

Con took his church duties very seriously indeed. At one wedding he officiated at two priests were helping but Con didn't need their interference. "Who's doing this wedding, me or you?" he admonished them. He was very well liked in the parish and one afternoon he took a young lad out in his car to a farm just outside Stockport for lunch and the boy saw more meat than he had ever seen before. The farmer had a gang of P.O.W.s working for him, just at the end of the War. Con also received a lot of petrol coupons for his car.

At confessions on a Saturday evening, some parishioners would insist in involving Con in gossip about boxing and some were in the confessional box for as long as thirty minutes. Those waiting outside for their turn must have thought that those inside had a lot of sins to confess.

Con hadn't much of a singing voice and his parish priest soon found that out, so at Midnight Mass on Christmas Eve 1946, Father Con was craftily kept off the altar by being asked by Father Molloy to "keep guard at the back of the Church" to discourage anyone who had had too much to drink beforehand from entering and causing a disturbance. Afterwards he asked "Did you have any trouble, Father Con?", whereupon Con smile and replied "Only with one guy, Father. I had to put this feller out of the church doors". "Oh, and did he go willingly?", asked Father Molloy. "Well, yes I think so. The ambulance soon came to collect him – I think they said he had suffered a fractured collar bone."

Con was living with his parents in Marple Road, Offerton, Stockport and Old Con died there on the morning of November 3rd 1947, when he was aged 61, happy in the knowledge that he had seen his son through three distinct phases of his eventful life – his amateur boxing days in Hull, his professional boxing career in England and America and then his priesthood days. He was buried in the family burial plot in Cork. After a happy twelve years or so in Stockport, Con was due for a change of parish and he was moved to the Star of the Sea Church, Ellesmere Port but he was not entirely happy there and after a year moved again, this time to Our Lady's Church (Immaculate Conception) in Birkenhead, where he became a legend and is still talked about in reverent terms over twenty years after his death. The parish was in the heart of dockland and Con again set up a boxing club for lads in the parish. Con became friendly with Johnny Campbell, the Liverpool boxing promoter who had Joe Bygraves under his control. Johnny would often ask Con to show Bygraves how to hit until one day Joe pleaded with Campbell "Don't let that tough assistant priest hit me again, boss. He really hurts with those digs!".

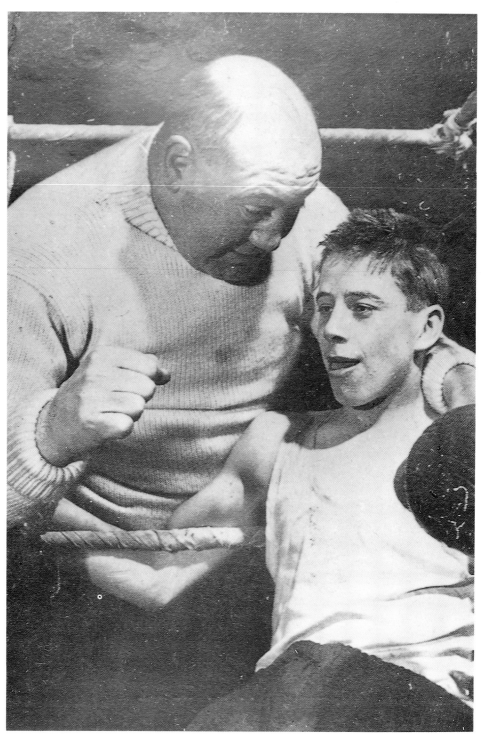

A young boxer receives advice from Father Con

Father Con on Bridlington sea front in 1952

Father Con didn't often return to his native city. He described it once to his housekeeper Mrs. Williams as "the city of bicycles" because of its flatness. One time he did come back he spent the Saturday evening touring local clubs appealing for contributions to help fund his boxing club. News spread quickly of his visit and Con was the centre of attraction throughout the night's tour. The very next morning Con preached at St. Charles' R.C. Church in Jarratt Street. A packed congregation heard him say "a lot of faces I see this morning I recognise and know they haven't been inside a Catholic Church for a long, long time. You haven't come to hear the words

69

Father Con, then Parish Priest at Church Stretton in Shropshire, returned to St. Charles' R.C. School in 1959. Boys Boxing Club member Tony Hindley receives some tips watched by (left to right) J. Sheridan, J. Kilkenny, Fr. J. Knowles and F. Hindley

Photo courtesy Hull Daily Mail

St. Patrick's Church in Dunmanway

St. Gabriel's Roman Catholic Church in Alsager, August 1988

of God from a priest, you've come to see an ex-boxer and that's wrong. You should have come to see and hear a Man of God".

Mrs. O'Kelly died in 1958 and she was buried in the family burial plot in Cork. While there, Con was out walking down the steep York Hill to say Mass at St. Patrick's Church when he fell awkwardly and twisted his knee very badly. An ambulance was called for and Con had to spend some time recuperating in hospital. Following his return to England, Con was moved to a new parish at St. Peter's in Stalybridge. He would often return to visit old friends and haunts at Bridlington and would take off his dog collar and drive up to Scarborough where he liked nothing better than to have a few whiskies and a good sing song. He liked to pose the question to his friends. "Am I like my dad?" and loved to hear the answer "Yes, but not as tall and you could never beat him!". He also took bunches of beautiful flowers to his mother's friends who still lived in the area.

He suffered great pain in his knees but remained ever-cheerful. He was now in charge of his own parish at St. Milburga Church in Church Stretton and though it was a tiny congregation who attended Mass there, Con was happy. His last parish was at St. Gabriels in Alsager where he lived in the house next to the Church. It was strongly rumoured at that time that Con had paid off the Church's debt with money made from his boxing career but could never be proved. In 1961 Teddy Ablett and his wife visited Con and found him in the middle of a group of young children. Teddy and Con had been at school at St. Charles together and Con had broken his nose in a playground incident. When he saw Teddy and his wife coming through the Church doors he recognised him and called "Now then Abo, how's your nose?!".

Con made many friends in the Alsager area, his down-to-earth manner proving to be very popular with his parishioners. He shunned publicity about his boxing career, turning down requests from National newspapers for his life story. Con died on a Sunday afternoon, September 8th, 1968 in a Nantwich hospital, aged 61. Coincidentally, it was the very week when the new St. Charles' R.C. school opened in Norfolk Street, Hull. He reputedly left his money and personal belongings to his housekeeper. The funeral was held at St. Joseph's Cemetery in Cork and Father Con was interred near his mother, father and sister.

Canon Wilfred Garlick wrote in tribute:- "I am very grieved to see in the newspapers of the death of an old friend, Father Con O'Kelly. He had a remarkable life as a pugilist before he became a Roman Catholic priest. I don't think he ever gave up being a 'pug' and one of my happiest memories was helping him 'sort out' a gang of young hooligans where his professional skill came in very useful. Con was a man among men and his cheerful manner and ready laugh made him very popular with his parishioners. He never aspired to be an exponent of involved theology. There was never the slightest danger of his becoming a Bishop or a dignitary. He was a simple man religiously but his Church was his birthright and he would defend it vigorously. Behind his huge frame there was a gentleness and humility which moved us more mightily than his strength. May he rest in peace".

A devoted life had come to an end – devotion to his family, devotion to boxing and finally and most important to Con, devotion to his religion.

CON O'KELLY – A CHAMPION AMONG CHAMPIONS

CON O'KELLY'S PROFESSIONAL BOXING CAREER DETAILS

1924

| Nov. 14 | Ike Clarke | W rsf 4 | Madeley Street Baths, Hull |
| Dec. 12 | Sonny Lonz Webster | W rsf 13 | Madeley Street Baths, Hull |

1925

Jan. 19	Ellis Powell	W rsf 5	Lyric Theatre, Hull
Feb. 2	Harry Moody	W rsf 7	Lyric Theatre, Hull
Feb. 16	Gunner Bennett	W dis 14	Lyric Theatre, Hull
Mar. 2	Stoker Stubbs	W ret 8	Lyric Theatre, Hull
Mar. 16	Trevor Llewellyn	W rsf 6	Lyric Theatre, Hull
Apr. 6	Stanley Glen	W ret 1	Lyric Theatre, Hull
May 7	Len Brookes	W dis 7	Liverpool Stadium
Sept. 28	George Hetherington	W dis 9	St. James' Hall, Newcastle
Oct. 5	Kid Moose	W pts 15	Artillery Barracks, Hull
Oct. 13	Dick Power	W ko 3	Free Trade Hall, Manchester
Oct. 21	Jack Phoenix	W rsf 4	St. George's Market, Belfast
Nov. 3	Harry Gold	W ko 1	Free Trade Hall, Manchester
Nov. 11	Charlie Chetwynd	L pts 15	Madeley Street Baths, Hull
Nov. 23	Joe Mullings	W rsf 3	National Sporting Club, London
Dec. 2	Jean Leroi	D 15	St. George's Market, Belfast
Dec. 15	Gunner Bennett	W dis 9	Free Trade Hall, Manchester

1926

Jan. 25	Jim McDonald	**W rsf 4**	National Sporting Club, London
Feb. 2	Paul Journee	**W rsf 2**	Madeley Street Baths, Hull
Feb. 16	Jean Leroi	**L pts 15**	Madeley Street Baths, Hull
Mar. 2	Jean Leroi	**W ko 5**	Madeley Street Baths, Hull
Mar. 22	Marine Trinder	**W rsf 8**	Madeley Street Baths, Hull
Apr. 30	Charlie Smith	**L pts 15**	Belle Vue, Manchester
Aug. 1	Stoker Stubbs	**W pts 15**	Leeds Stadium
Oct. 18	Stoker Stubbs	**W ko 9**	York
Oct. 30	George Hetherington	**W ko 3**	Bridlington Spa
Nov. 15	Dave Magill	**L ret 11**	Madeley Street Baths, Hull

1927

Jan. 17	Stoker Miller	**W pts 15**	Cleethorpes
Feb. 7	Gus Platts	**W pts 15**	Madeley Street Baths, Hull
Feb. 18	Tom Fowler	**W ko 4**	Scunthorpe
Feb. 25	Fred Young	**W ko 1**	Central Room, Bridlington Spa
Mar. 14	Will Lancaster	**W ret 6**	York
Mar. 30	Ted Sandwina	**D 10**	Royal Albert Hall, London
May 5	Gunner Bennett	**W rsf 4**	Royal Albert Hall, London
Jun. 2	Ted Sandwina	**L pts 15**	Royal Albert Hall, London
Aug. 23	John Strand	**W rsf 11**	Metropole, Hull
Oct. 24	Battling Sullivan	**W ret 3**	Victoria Baths, Nottingham
Nov. 7	Dave Magill	**W rsf 6**	Madeley Street Baths, Hull
Nov. 28	Roland Todd	**D 15**	Madeley Street Baths, Hull

1928

Jan. 16	Tom Berry	W pts 15	Madeley Street Baths, Hull
Jan. 30	Van Der Veer	W pts 15	National Sporting Club, London
Feb. 6	Harry Crossley	D 15	Madeley Street Baths, Hull
Feb. 27	Leon Sebilo	W rsf 10	Madeley Street Baths, Hull
Mar. 19	Jack Stanley	W ko 7	Madeley Street Baths, Hull
Nov. 5	Al Friedman	W pts 10	Madison Square Gardens, New York
Nov. 23	Jack Gagnon	W pts 10	Mechanic Buildings, Philadelphia
Dec. 21	Jim Maloney	D 10	Madison Square Gardens, New York

1929

Jan. 25	George Gemas	W rsf 3	Syracuse
Feb. 1	Jim Maloney	L pts 10	Boston Gardens
Feb. 15	Ernie Schaaf	W dis 6	Boston Gardens
Mar. 4	Matt Adgie	L pts 10	The Arena, Philadelphia
Apr. 8	Harold Mays	L pts 10	The Arena, Philadelphia
Apr. 19	Jim Maloney	L rsf 3	Madison Square Gardens, New York

1930

Jun. 17	Jack Dudley	W ko 7	Portland Maine
Aug. 19	Tiger Tom Dixon	W ko 8	Portland Maine
Sep. 30	King Solomon	W pts 12	Portland Maine
Oct. 21	Jack Gagnon	L pts 10	Boston Arena
Dec. 15	Al Friedman	W pts 10	Boston Arena

1931

Jan. 30	Michele Bonaglia	**W dis 3**	New Jersey
Mar. 31	King Levinsky	**L pts 10**	Boston Arena
May 5	Harold Mays	**No dec. 6**	Portland Maine
Jul. 13	Giacomo Bergomas	**D 10**	Madison Square Gardens, New York
Aug. 10	Giacomo Bergoma	**L pts 10**	Madison Square Gardens
Aug. 24	Tuffy Griffiths	**L pts 10**	Chicago
Sep. 9	King Levinsky	**D 10**	Chicago
Sep. 25	Dick Daniels	**L pts 10**	Minneapolis
Oct. 26	Baxter Calmes	**L pts 10**	Chicago

1932-1936

Semi-retirement

1937

Sep. 22	Bert Ikin	**W ret 3**	White City, Hull
Oct. 6	Max Hodgetts	**W ret 5**	White City, Hull
Dec. 1	Jacob Schonrath	**W pts 10**	Liverpool Stadium

1938

Jan. 25	Harry Lister	**W pts 15**	Free Trade Hall, Manchester
	(Vacant Northern Area Heavyweight Title)		
Feb. 17	Erwin Klein	**W pts 10**	Liverpool Stadium
Mar. 24	Cal Rooney	**W pts 8**	Anfield Stadium, Liverpool